# SETTING

## Creative Visualization For Healing

*Alan Cohen*

**To order** *Setting the Seen*

**Personal Orders:**
To order by Visa, MasterCard, or American Express, call:
**1 (800) 462-3013**
*Toll-free number for orders and catalog requests only.*

Or write:

ALAN COHEN PUBLICATIONS
P.O. Box 98509
Des Moines, WA 98198

For a free catalog of Alan Cohen's books, tapes and workshop schedule, write or call the address or telephone number above.

**Bookstore Orders:**

*Setting the Seen* is available from these distributors of fine inspirational books:

| | |
|---|---|
| Aquarian Book Dist. | Ingram Book Company |
| Baker & Taylor | Moving Books |
| Bookpeople | New Leaf Distributing Co. |
| De Vorss & Co. | Whole Health Book Co. |

This guide is suggested as a companion to the stereo audio-cassette, *Peace,* by Alan Cohen, with musical soundtrack by Steven Halpern. Most of the guided visualizations in this book are narrated on the cassette, with background music appropriate for each selection.

# BY ALAN COHEN

## *Books*
Companions of the Heart
The Dragon Doesn't Live Here Anymore
Have You Hugged A Monster Today?
　　with illustrations by Keith Kelly
The Healing of the Planet Earth
Joy Is My Compass
The Peace That You Seek
Rising In Love
Setting the Seen

## *Cassette Tapes*
Deep Relaxation
　　with music by Steven Halpern
Eden Morning
I Believe In You
　　with songs & music by  Stephen Longfellow Fiske
Miracle Mountain
Peace
　　with music by Steven Halpern

## *Video*
Dare To Be Yourself

# TABLE OF CONTENTS

*An introduction to the power of creative visualization* . . . . . . . . . . . . . . iv

*How to use this manual* . . . . . . . . . . . . . . . . . . . . . . . . . . . . . . . . 1

## The Images

I FREEMIND — *To stimulate imagination and creativity* . . . . . . . . 3

II PAIRED FANTASIES — *To encourage creative sharing
in a group* . . . . . . . . . . . . . . . . . . . . . . . . . . . . . . . . . . . 5

III FOCUSING — *To develop concentration and mental imagery* . . 7

IV THE PEACEFUL ME — *For deep relaxation and
stress reduction*\* . . . . . . . . . . . . . . . . . . . . . . . . . . . . . . . . . 9

V EXPANDING LIGHT — *To strengthen positive thinking* . . . . . . . 11

VI THE LAKE AND THE LADDER — *To soothe and calm
the emotions*\* . . . . . . . . . . . . . . . . . . . . . . . . . . . . . . . . . . 13

VII THE GIFT OF HEALING — *For physical healing*\* . . . . . . . . . . . 15

VIII RAINBOW WATERFALL — *To deepen sensitivity to the healing
effects of color*\* . . . . . . . . . . . . . . . . . . . . . . . . . . . . . . . . 18

IX WHO AM I? — *For calm detachment and mental clarity*\* . . . . . . 20

X GUIDING STAR — *To nurture trust and self-esteem* . . . . . . . . 22

XI HELPING HANDS — *To enhance the quality of
human services*\* . . . . . . . . . . . . . . . . . . . . . . . . . . . . . . . . 24

XII CIRCLE OF LOVE — *For healing relationships*\* . . . . . . . . . . . . 26

*Suggestions for background music and other reference materials* . . . . . 29

\*Narrated with music on cassette tape, PEACE (see pg. ii)

# An Introduction to the Power of Creative Visualization

There is a creative power in the mind that offers unlimited possibilities to all of us. This potential has been virtually unused, except by those great ones we laud as geniuses, inventors, and heroes. The irony — and the promise — of this important ability is that it is certainly not restricted to those who have discovered its value; it is available to you and me in equal measure. We can all experience deep relaxation, health, abundance, love, and peace of mind to the extent that we are willing to channel our imaginative abilities in the proper way.

The essence of the power of creative visualization is this simple formula:

*SEE WHAT YOU WANT TO BE.*

To put it more practically, *if you want to be something in life* — such as more relaxed, clear, or loving — *you must first get a mental vision of your ideal self, and then nurture this picture with positive thoughts.* This blueprint for personal growth has been demonstrated many times over in my life, and I stand behind it with the deepest confidence.

The purpose of this book is to enable you to make use of this important principle in your personal and professional life. Ideas are only as useful as they are practical, and the images in this guide will prove their worth as you experiment with them. Each of the visualizations is intended to develop a specific experience of tranquility, according to your need or that of your client.

The applications of creative visualization are as boundless as the aspects of personal growth, and you are encouraged to use the guided images here as a starting point from which you can develop your own personal mental imagery.

It was Jonathan Livingston Seagull's teacher who put it very simply:

*"Begin by knowing that you've already arrived"*

*Alan Cohen*

# HOW TO USE THIS MANUAL

This booklet is a series of guided mental images — mind pictures — which can create positive changes in mental, emotional, and physical well-being. These images have been demonstrated to be powerful tools for personal growth, and this guide is a handbook for personal and professional use of the techniques.

The manual includes suggestions for teachers, counselors, and persons in the helping and healing professions who would like to bring about deeper relaxation, heightened creativity, and improved health in students, clients, or patients.

You may use these processes for yourself, with individuals, or with groups. You are free (and encouraged!) to adapt the exercises to apply to your particular students or clients, for these images are most effective when they are tailored to your students' personal interests and aspirations.

Here are some general suggestions for presenting the material:

1. Use a quiet place and time when you will be free from interruptions or distractions.

2. It is preferable not to do these processes right after eating a meal.

3. Have students sit comfortably upright with their feet on the floor (not crossed). Heads should not droop or tilt. Processes may also be done while lying down.

4. Speak *slowly* and *clearly*, allowing a great deal of time for students to picture and absorb the images as you guide them. Use your intuition to place pauses and spaces where they are necessary. (. . .) in the text indicates an important pause.

5. It is very important that you picture the images as you are presenting them. This will help you to create an atmosphere that supports the students' visualization, and enable you to facilitate the sharing after the experience.

6. Allow at least five minutes after the process before the students must get up or leave.

7. Take time after each process for students to share what they have experienced. It is not necessary to interpret or understand the students' experience. Simply encourage them to describe and share.

8. The suggested background musical selections are very helpful, but not necessary. Feel free to use whatever selections you find appropriate. It is possible to do the exercises without music, but I have found the music to be extremely valuable.

9. It is best not to do more than one process per session.

# I. FREEMIND

*To stimulate imagination and creativity.*

Close your eyes and take three deep breaths . . . Let your body settle in, and feel your emotions become quiet . . . Keep breathing deeply and relax . . .

Now is an opportunity for you to fantasize, to let your mind picture and play out anything you wish. As I speak, begin to picture yourself doing anything you would just love to do, no matter how "unrealistic" it may seem. This is your chance to be daring and adventurous and to see yourself in ways far greater than your usual picture of who you believe you are. Now there are absolutely no limitations on what you may do in your fantasy. Do not restrict or inhibit yourself in any way. Let your mind be completely free to imagine whatever you wish . . .

Think of all the things that you have always wanted to do — your secret ambitions, dreams, and aspirations — and visualize yourself doing them right now. One by one, let the images appear and create a mental movie of which you are the star. See all the scenes in living color and notice as many details as you can . . . As the producer and director, you can picture and experience anything you decide . . .

Because your mind is not limited by time or by space, you can go anywhere in the world — or the universe. You can be rich, famous, and beautiful . . . You can be an inventor, a movie star, a sports hero, or a great statesman. You can travel to another planet, or to the dawn of civilization. You can walk the Parthenon in ancient Greece, or live in a crystal house in the twenty-fourth century. You are completely free to be whatever you wish. Whatever you want to be, in your deepest dreams, be it now. Whatever you want to do, in your most thrilling fantasies, do it now. See it all in striking detail, and enjoy yourself.

*Pause 1 minute.*

Good. Now, are you really letting go? Are you still restricting or stopping yourself in any way? Is there anything you think you can't do or be? If there is, fantasize that now. Leave nothing unpictured. Let your mind create in even greater detail.

*Pause 1 minute.*

You now have one minute left. Really let go now. See if there are any fantasies you would still like to enjoy. Look deep into yourself and see if there are any wishes, dreams, or aspirations that you have thought about, but not done or told anyone. Now is your time to experience them in your mental movie. Make the colors vivid. Listen clearly to the words or sounds. Make it very real, and exaggerate each idea.

*Pause 1 minute.*

Very good. Now begin to wind down your fantasies. Slowly and purposefully conclude your mental picturing, and begin to return to this room . . . *(sufficient pause)* . . . Good. As you are ready, slowly open your eyes . . .

*Allow sufficient time for transition.*

Who would like to tell what you experienced? You do not need to say what your fantasies were, but let's share what it felt like to fantasize like this . . .

*After several participants have spoken:*

Who would like to tell what you fantasized?

# II. PAIRED FANTASIES

*To develop confidence to share creatively in a group.*

Participants should be sitting in pairs, facing each other.

You and your partner are now going to have a chance to make up a story together. Would one of you from each pair now raise your hand? . . . Thank you. You who raised your hand will be storyteller A, and your partner, B. When I say "Begin" (or ring a bell), person A will begin to make up a story. The story can be about any idea or theme, true or fictitious. The most important element is to make the story and its characters as fascinating and captivating as possible. See what an intriguing storyteller you can be.

When I say "Change" (or ring a bell), person A must stop exactly where you are — even in the middle of a sentence — and person B will continue where A left off. Stay with the same story line, and keep it interesting and exciting. See how you can embellish the story that A began. Then when I say "Change" (ring bell) again, B must stop right where you are, and A will pick it up from that exact point. Keep the tale going in this way, changing when I say so, until I tell you to stop.

Ready? . . . Person A: Begin.

*Vary the amount of time each interval. One interval may be a minute, and the next fifteen seconds, etc. Give each partner four or five turns. After about ten minutes:*

Now begin to wrap up your story and bring it to a satisfying resolution. A will get one more chance, and B will then conclude the story.

*Processing: Give each pair a few minutes to share with each other what they experienced as they were creating the tale. Then open up the sharing to the entire group. Have each pair (if small group), or some pairs (if large group) give a **short** synopsis of their story.*

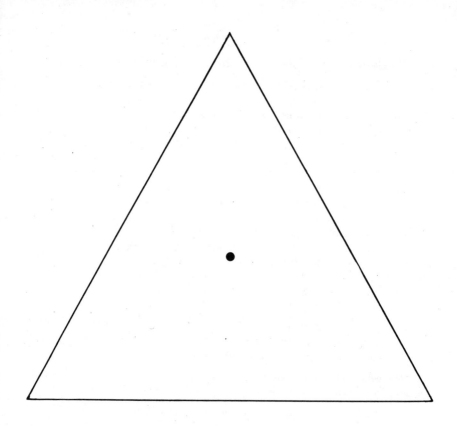

*You may use this illustration to practice focusing by yourself or with a small group. For larger groups, you may draw the diagram on a blackboard or poster paper. It is also possible to do the exercise without the diagram, simply visualizing the image with closed eyes.*

# III. FOCUSING

## To develop concentration and mental imagery.

*These three images are recommended as a warm-up to the longer, deeper visualizations that follow.*

I will now suggest to you some interesting images. They are intended to strengthen your concentraion and test your ability to focus on and experience a clear image.

### 1

We will start with a simple geometric figure — a triangle with a dot in the middle. Look directly at this dot, and for the next two minutes keep your eyes and your concentration completely upon it.

*Give these instructions at intervals during the two minutes.*

Stay with the dot . . . Concentrate with a firm, yet relaxed attitude . . You can do it if you set your mind to it . . . If your mind wanders, bring it back to the point . . . Your only job is to stay with the point . . . Make your mind very clear and sharp . . . Focus more clearly, now, as if you could look even more deeply into the center of that dot . . . Stay with it . . . Let nothing distract you . . . Hold for just a few more moments . . .

Very good. Now stop looking at that dot and relax your eyes. As you are ready, bring your attention back to me and this group . . . *(sufficient pause)* . . .

Who was able to stay with the dot for the whole time? . . . Who had a hard time concentrating? . . . What does it feel like to have your mind concentrated? . . . How is it different than having your mind scattered or vague? . . . In what ways could more concentration help you?

### 2

Now let's take another image: a red rose. Close your eyes and in your mind's eye, see a beautiful, vibrant red rose. Focus your mind intently on that rose and nothing else. See if you can keep your mind on the rose and only the rose for the next two minutes.

Look at all the details of the rose . . . How big is it? . . . What shade of red do you see? . . . Keep the rose clearly in the center of your mental vision . . . How many petals does this vibrant rose have? . . . In what stage of unfoldment is it? . . . Is this rose fully open, or is it just a bud? . . . Do you see any dew drops on it? . . . Take the remaining moments to see all of the other details of this rose . . . *(extended pause)* . . .

Now, as you keep focusing on the rose, become aware of the feelings the rose evokes within you. What sort of mood does the rose put you in? . . . What kind of energy does it give you? . . . Does it soothe you? . . . Does it make you feel loving? . . . Feel what the rose does for you and allow these feelings to expand within you. Keep concentrating and feeling . . . *(extended pause)* . . .

Good. Now slowly let the rose and the feelings fade from your inner vision and your experience.

### 3

Now we will take another image: moonlight on the snow. It is a deep winter's evening, just after a snowfall, and you are walking down a winding country road. The air is crisp and you smell the smoke from a fireplace down the road. As you come around a bend, you find yourself before a vast, open field, covered with freshly fallen snow . . . See how smooth and perfect is the surface of the snow, and how delicate is its soft texture . . . Now look up and see a bright white full moon in a clear sky. See how the moon is shining over the whole open field, and it seems as if every snowflake is glimmering in the reflection of the light of the moon. It's a rare and beautiful scene . . . (*extended pause*) . . .

Now feel the mood of the scene . . . Experience the serenity and the quietness. Though the air is chilly and you can see your breath, there is a warm glow in your heart, like the mellow contentment of a wood fire in a stove. Feel the wonder of the scene as you sit quietly with this soothing picture and absorb it . . . (*extended pause*) . . . Good. Now, as you are ready, slowly open your eyes and return your awareness to this room.

# IV. THE PEACEFUL ME

*For deep relaxation and reducing stress.*

Remember to give participants ample time to focus and relax.

Close your eyes and take a few deep breaths . . . *(ample pause)* . . . Let's begin by allowing our feet to relax. As you focus your attention on your feet, feel how nice it is for all the muscles in your toes and feet to be loose and easy . . . It's a very natural feeling . . . Now let go of your legs in the same way, noticing how all of the muscles and nerves enjoy your letting go . . . In the same way, release your buttocks and hips; let all of these muscles sink comfortably into your chair . . . It's a very pleasant feeling . . . This is your time to refresh yourself and renew your energy . . . *(extended pause)* . . .

Now pay attention to your back. Notice how you can sit up straight and still be at ease . . . See if you are holding any muscles tight. This tension is not necessary now, and so you can let it go. As your back is becoming more and more relaxed, feel the flow of energy moving through your spine. Feel how the same energy flows through your chest and especially through your lungs. Take a few more deep breaths as you distribute this soothing energy throughout your whole body. Feel what it means to breathe free and easy . . .

This peaceful feeling spreads naturally to your shoulders and neck. You can let go of your shoulders now. Let any troubles or burdens just slide off of you, so your shoulders are left very loose and easy. It's a wonderful feeling to be relaxed. Experience the difference between stress and relaxation. If you like, shrug your shoulders up to your ears and hold them there tightly, to exaggerate any tension in your neck. Hold for about ten seconds, and then let go. *(Give ten seconds)* . . . Now drop your shoulders and let your neck be completely free of any tightness . . . See how easily this relaxed feeling spreads to your arms and hands, down through your fingers, until you can even feel the muscles and nerves in your fingers relaxing . . . Enjoy these pleasant feelings . . .

Now bring your awareness to your face. See if you are holding your jaw tight. If so, let it go. Sometimes we are holding tension that we are not even aware of, until we let it go. Notice if you are holding your forehead taut, in a squint or frown. If so, let these muscles go. Slowly and carefully go over the different parts of your face, and one by one let them ease up. See how open and radiant you can allow your face to be. Let your whole head be completely loose, as if a warm hand is gently brushing over your forehead, leaving it completely open and smooth.

Now let your whole body go, as if you are a big fluffy sponge . . . That's it . . . You are a channel for soothing energy to flow easily, and each breath brings you into deeper peace and tranquility . . .

Now let your mind scan your memories, until you come to a time in your life when you were very relaxed. Perhaps it was during a special vacation . . . or while you were enjoying one of your favorite interests . . . or during a warm moment with good friends . . . or when you were in love . . . Tune into the scene very clearly, as if you are watching a movie of the experience. Remember what you were doing at that peaceful time . . . who you were with . . . and how it felt. Now re-

9

experience what you were feeling then, as if you are right there, as if it is happening right now. See the nicest details of the scene. Feel the peace in your body. What is the expression on your face? . . . What is the tone of your muscles? . . . Experience all the positive emotions and the contentment, and feel it now . . . A deep inner peace . . . A trust . . . A love for life . . . Feel the safety and confidence in yourself that makes this moment special. Feel, too, the ease and peacefulness that is very much a part of you.

Once again get to know the peaceful "me." It's a calm me, an O.K. me, an easy-going me. It's the real me. Isn't this the me that you would like to be all the time? Feel how right it feels to be the peaceful me. It's a joyous feeling, a rewarding feeling, an encouraging feeling . . . Now take a few moments to enjoy the peaceful me. Notice how your body is sitting, how your emotions are calm, how your mind is clear, and how positive you are. I now introduce you to the peaceful me . . .

Now visualize the peaceful me in the midst of your present activities. Choose one area of your life in which you would like to experience the peaceful me. Perhaps it's your job . . . or your family . . . or your relationships . . . How would it feel if the peaceful me were really functioning in this area? . . . Visualize the peaceful me in this aspect of your life, going through all the activities in a completely easy and positive way . . . Fantasize how successful and rewarding this activity is. Notice how your state of ease makes you effective in accomplishing exactly what you want . . . Watch a mental movie of the peaceful me in action . . . See how you are standing . . . walking . . . and sitting. Hear how calmly you speak and how openly you listen . . . Notice the poise and balance in your movements . . . Now observe the positive feedback you are receiving from your friends and coworkers. See yourself smiling and satisfied. Create all of the details of the peaceful me, and watch the most rewarding scene you can imagine . . . (extended pause) . . .

Good. Now, we are going to begin to return our awareness to this room. As you are ready, begin to open your eyes. Take your time; go at your own pace. Remember that you do not have to stop being the peaceful me; you can stay this way, calm and serene, as long as you like, even as you re-enter activity. Your relaxed self is very real now; you have reawakened it . . . Take a few deep breaths, and slowly begin to wiggle your toes and move your fingers. Take some more deep breaths and allow your eyes to open slowly. As they open, look at the room in a new and relaxed way — through the eyes of the peaceful me.

# V. EXPANDING LIGHT
*To develop positive thinking and creativity.*

Visualize a candle about three feet in front of you. It's a long, white, perfectly straight candlestick, with a bright flame on top of it. Look at the flame with a firm but comfortable gaze. See if you can find the brightest spot within the flame, the brilliant light at the center, right at the tip of the wick. Focus your attention on that bright spot and keep your attention right there. Look more deeply into the light with each breath . . . See if you can find the center of the flame that does not flicker . . . If your mind wanders to something else, gently bring it back to that bright, calm center. Keep looking into the center of the flame . . . *(ample pause)* . . .

Good. Now mentally bring that flame into the center of your forehead, right above your nose. See if you can locate it perfectly in the middle of your forehead and look up at it. Now place that light in the very center of your head. As you locate it there, feel waves and rays of light emanating from the center, filling your entire head with a peaceful warmth. Feel how the energy from this light has a soothing and healing effect on your whole head . . .

When your head is completely filled with light, bring this beautiful flame down into your chest, and place it in the center of your heart. Let the light expand, pouring through your entire torso, completely filling all of your organs with brilliant energy. Let the light go into every space. Feel the warmth and completeness of this lovely light . . .

Now let the light continue to pour through your arms, radiating all the way to your hands and your fingertips. It's as if the light just wants to expand and to make everything it touches feel good . . .

In the same way, let this beautiful light pour down through your legs and your feet, making them feel new and alive. It's a wonderful, wonderful feeling for you to enjoy.

When your entire body is filled with light, see how this light wants to continue to expand, even beyond the limits of your skin. And you can let it. Imagine the light pouring out to the left of you, first a few inches, now a few feet, and now let it stream out as far as you can imagine. Forget about my voice, forget about any other people in the room, forget about everything. Just feel the brilliance of this wonderous light. Imagine there are no walls, and see how far you can see this sparkling light streaming out to the left of you.

Now let the light pour out to the right of you in the same way. It's so easy. Just let it flow . . . Feel it radiate a few inches, then a few feet, then many, many feet, until the light is so brilliant that you can't even see the right side of your body. Now let it go beyond where the walls were, and watch it keep going as far as your mind can imagine.

Now let the light pour out in front of you, too, way, way out. Make it brighter with your mind. Enjoy the energy of it. All you can see in front of you is wonderous light, as all things have been replaced by light.

Now let the light pour out behind you, as far as you can think. That's very, very far. This light is shining from the center of your self, a center that becomes only stronger and brighter as you think of it.

11

Now pour the light below you, as if the floor has disappeared . . . and above you, as if there is no ceiling, until everywhere you look you see only radiant splendor. It is as if you are sitting in the middle of the sun, and everywhere is only peaceful light.

Now enjoy this clear space. This is a free space, in which all things are quiet and free and at peace. Here is a resting place for you, a tranquil retreat into open space. Stay here as long as you like, and experience light . . . (*extended pause*). . .

Good. Now, as you are ready, begin to be aware of your physical body again. You do not have to let go of the light to be aware of your body; you can actually draw the light into your body and take the light with you. Gradually notice your head, your torso, arms, and legs. Notice the position of your fingers and toes, and feel the texture of the chair or floor. Slowly, now, open your eyes and readjust yourself to this room.

*After ample time:*

Who would like to tell what you experienced as you focused on the light?

# VI. THE LAKE AND THE LADDER
## *To soothe and calm the emotions.*

Visualize before you a tranquil and placid mountain lake. See how there is not a ripple on the surface of the water. The lake is a perfect mirror. Look at the reflection of the mountains on the still surface of the lake, and see how the white fluffy clouds in the blue sky are exactly mirrored on the water. The entire scene is one of absolute tranquility. Now, with your mind, ripple the water a bit. Make a few little waves and watch the ripples go out over the whole lake, so the reflection is distorted. Now, with your mind, bring the surface of the water back to tranquility so the lake is as calm and perfectly serene as it was . . .

Now, because anything is possible in the mind, visualize a ladder in the center of the lake. See a long golden ladder that reaches up from the surface of the lake through an opening in the clouds . . . Now step onto the surface of the lake, and because you are creating this scene and you can do what you like in it, you find that you can actually walk just a few inches above the water. To your happy surprise, you are light and airy.

Now walk to the base of the ladder. You can actually do it; in your mind you can do anything. As you reach the base of this majestic golden ladder, look up at the portal at the top of the ladder and see the most beautiful radiant golden light. It is warm and inviting, and it makes you just want to climb up the ladder and feel more of the light. Go ahead. Take a step up the ladder . . . now another . . . and another. That's good. Keep climbing slowly and steadily, feeling more and more of this amazing light as you ascend. You find your climb becoming easier as you go higher . . . All you want to do now is enter that golden light and feel it all around you. Come up a little higher now, and a little more. You are now very close to the top. As you approach the opening, feel the light pouring through you in waves of healing energy more wonderful than you ever thought possible.

Now raise your head through the clouds and enter the realm of golden light. It seems to be shining everywhere you look. It flows over your head and your face, bathing you in soothing peace. Keep rising until you are completely above the clouds, standing in a new world of lovely peacefulness. It is like a warm bath of bliss, perhaps as you felt as a little child. Look all around and feel it. There is no one here but you. You can stand naked, with open arms, and accept the healing energy that is pouring all over your body from all directions . . .

As your body is soothed by this healing balm, feel that you are getting lighter and lighter, and your whole body is beginning to absorb this wonderful energy. Imagine every cell of you drinking up this light until you are sparkling inside and out. Feel as if you are actually merging into this light . . . You are becoming this light that you love . . . You *are* the peacefulness that you sought . . . *(extended pause)* . . . Stay in this joyfulness as it becomes a real part of your self . . .

Now, filled with light, we are going to return to the top of the ladder, taking the light with us. Step on the first rung, just above the clouds, and with a sense of completeness in your heart, begin to step down, rung by rung. To your happy discovery, you find that the feeling of the light is staying with you; it *has* become a part of you. Continue slowly, now, descending rung by rung until you arrive at the surface of the lake, where you turn and face the shore from which you began your journey into light. Now walk once again over the surface of the water and return to the shore . . .

Standing on the shore, see before you the great panorama of all creation, one that you did not notice before. See the trees of the forest . . . the flowers . . . the animals . . . and the birds. See, too, the great valley, with its cities of people and activity. You have an overflowing abundance of energy to share. Feel how natural it is to give what you have received. Mentally open your arms, smile, and radiate the feeling that you have . . . Give it to everything you see, and know that all who come into your thoughts receive a great gift. Pour your light, your love, and your energy to all of creation. You have a special treasure to share — an unlimited flow of life and happiness. There is a world of people waiting for your peace, and a universal gift that you are ready to share.

# VII. THE GIFT OF HEALING
## For physical healing.

*This image is very powerful for physical healing. It is especially effective when done while lying in bed before going to sleep. Regular practice of this visualization for five minutes each night will greatly enhance the healing process in the body.*

Take three very deep breaths and feel that you are releasing all thoughts and tensions from the day. With each inbreath visualize clear, pure, healing energy filling your chest, and with each outbreath imagine any stress or negativity being completely expelled from your system. Do this as long as you need, until you feel that you have flushed out your system and filled yourself with light . . . (*extended pause*) . . .

Now inhale deeply, and as you exhale imagine that you are pouring healing energy down your left leg. Visualize your left leg as hollow, and as you breathe you are completely filling it with health and life. Repeat this healing breath, making sure to energize the whole leg, right down to the tips of your toes. Feel that your leg is open and porous, like a sponge, and it gladly accepts the wholeness you are channeling to it. One more time inhale deeply, hold the breath energy in your chest for a few seconds, and then flow it down your left leg, as if you are infusing it with a perfect pattern that all of the atoms, cells and organs can form around. Feel, too, that your left leg is surrounded for a few inches with a fluffy, white light, like a substance of health energy . . .

Now turn your attention to the right leg and breathe into it. Charge it with energy and light. Offer it three healing breaths, until it feels balanced and radiant, like the left leg . . . (*sufficient pause*) . . . After your third breath, experience how wonderful and alive your legs feel, as if they are brand new . . .

When your legs are completely filled with light, give energy to your left arm. Breathe into it as if it is a sponge. As you pour sparkling light into it, it becomes fluffy and open. Breathe into it again, and see how it seems to expand more with each breath. Make sure to pour the energy into your fingers and hands, right down to the fingertips. See how fulfilled your arm becomes as you give it your loving attention in three breaths . . .

Energize your right arm now, and see how it loosens up and has a kind of floating sensation as you breathe three times into it. Experience the wonderful strength in the right arm, and feel a healing flow of peaceful life energize it right into your fingertips. Feel, too, how flexible and alive are your fingers. It is a marvelous and peaceful feeling. You can even surround your right arm with an aura of healthy vitality, as your energy field extends beyond your physical body.

Now turn your attention to the left side of your torso, breathing life into all of the organs from your shoulders to your hips. Think of the organs that live within you: your heart, your left lung, your spleen. Feel that these organs are your friends, and that you can help them and make them happy by giving them your positive attention. Take a deep breath, and as you exhale fill the entire left side of your torso with healing light. Visualize all of the organs accepting this gift with gratefulness and enthusiasm. Again, breathe into the left side, this time filling the organs with yet deeper and more subtle energy, as if the energy from your breath could just seep deep, deep into your cells, like a healing balm that finds its way into even the smallest spaces. Finally take one more breath and imagine that you are sending energy into the tiniest cells, and even into the very atoms of your body. Feel how wonderful and peaceful it is to be healthy and alive . . .

Now focus on the right side of your torso, which is joyous to receive your attention. Consider the right lung, the liver, and the kidneys. Now give them your loving breath. Breathe three times to the right side, at your own pace, and feel the life and love within yourself. Know that you are doing your body a great service, and that the results of this attention will make themselves known to you in the form of health and happiness. Concentrate very clearly, and allow the natural healing process to work within you. Your natural state is health, and now you are rightfully claiming it.

Give your attention now to your shoulders. If you have had any stress or tension in your shoulders or neck, now is your opportunity to let it go. Take a deep breath and pour your loving peace into all of the muscles in your neck. Keep breathing and imagine that two firm, yet gentle, warm hands are resting on your shoulders, and the energy from these hands is steadily and surely flowing into all the muscles in your neck, coating all the nerves with a balm of quiet restfulness. Stay with your shoulders and keep giving them gentle breaths as long as you need to let them be completely at ease.

Now bring your awareness to your head. Notice if you are holding any tension or tightness here. Are you keeping your jaw tight? Are you wrinkling your forehead? Is your scalp tight? If so, now is your moment to let it all go. Very gently take a deep breath and breathe it to the left side of your face and head. Feel a soothing peacefulness rolling through your left eye, cheek, and ear. This wave of ease releases any remnants of stress on this side of your head. Experience how nice and peaceful it is to be free of tension and relaxed . . .

Do the same, now, for the right side of your head. Your right cheek, eye, ear, and temple are waiting for your soothing breath. Feel these parts of yourself respond as you give them what they need . . .

Now breathe once to the front of your face. Focus especially on the eyes and the muscles that support them. Visualize the eyes resting peacefully in their perfect place, and feel the energy flowing from the brain through the optic nerve to the eyes. Feel how smooth and soft is your forehead, like a little baby's. See your face as radiant and bright . . .

Now breathe softly to the back of your head. There are many important glands and organs at the base of your skull, and now you can help them renew themselves and function perfectly. Feel a wonderful flow of peaceful light through the back of your head and allow it to rest perfectly and gently just as it is.

Now bring your awareness to your brain. The brain controls all the other bodily functions. As you energize the brain you heal every single cell of your body. Very gently breathe loving light into your brain, with a deep appreciation for the marvelous work that it does. Thank it for the amazing way it keeps you whole, a function far more miraculous than any human being has ever been able to comprehend. This is your moment to express your gratefulness by breathing love and peace into it. This is your moment for complete health . . . (*extended pause*) . . . Continue to breathe deeply and slowly, until your entire body rests in a happy, peaceful feeling, and you know that you are a wonderful, whole, alive person. You have now claimed and experienced the complete health that is rightfully yours.

# VIII. RAINBOW WATERFALL
*For deepening sensitivity to the healing effects of color*
*This visualization is especially effective when experienced while lying down.*

Close your eyes and let your body go . . . Imagine before you a beautiful, bright rainbow, more dazzling and breathtaking than you have ever seen. See all of the colors, lucid and clear. Perhaps you can even see an essence, a vibration in each of the colors, a radiance that you usually do not see. These are very pure colors.

Now allow one of these sparkling colors to become brighter, calling to you as if it wants you to pay special attention to it . . . This may be your favorite color, or it may not . . . Take this bright and sharp color and mentally place it over your head. As it vibrates above you, imagine that this color is turning into a liquid light, and this light is beginning to flow down toward you like a magical mountain waterfall . . . and you are like a mountain stream.

Feel your color flowing into the top of your head. It's a good feeling, a soothing feeling, one that brings much peacefulness. Feel this healing color flow into the center of your head, gently easing all of the nerves and cells that it touches. It is bringing a very joyful experience with it. How nice it feels as your color begins to flow through your face! It washes away any tightness or tension in your forehead, leaving your brow smooth and fresh. Now your whole head is taking on the radiant aura of this lovely color.

See if you can discover and feel the healing essence of your color. Every color brings a healing experience. See what your color does for you . . .

Now allow your beautiful color to flow down through your shoulders and arms. There is a richness in this color that you have not noticed before. It is getting stronger and brighter, rushing and gushing through all the passageways in your body. It is as if it wants to fill you up and wash away all tensions. Let your torso absorb this light energy until you are fully flowing and alive. Feel how it massages and softens all of your inner organs, leaving them fresh and vibrant . . . This is a gentle but powerful energy. See your color quietly filling your muscles and cells, and imagine that this special light finds its way even into your atoms. Watch how subtle and fine is the work that this color is doing . . .

Now feel this energy cascade through your abdomen and hips, and then let it flow down through your legs. Feel as if your legs are open channels, like the hollows in the side of a mountain that make space for crystal waters to flow down into the valley. It's an easy feeling, a light feeling, a satisfied feeling. Notice how the mountain waterfall has washed away any stress that you started with, leaving you free and fresh and open . . .

Finally let this liquid light flow out the bottoms of your feet, as if you are providing an outlet for the light to continue flowing. You are a vessel, a channel, a space. Every part of you is open and breathing and peaceful . . .

Now something very fascinating is going to happen. As the liquid light pours out of the bottoms of your feet, it is going to return to the top of your head, recycling itself in a marvelous circle of light that has only one purpose: to bring healing energy through your body. Let it happen. Experience all that it brings to you . . . With each breath, let your color penetrate into a new depth of your being . . . into your physical body, through your emotions, and even into your mind. The light is so subtle that it is affecting you and helping you on the quietest levels. Enjoy it. You are clear. You are radiant. You are sparkling. You are as fresh and alive as the brightest mountain stream.

Be that open vessel, like a flute, and let mother nature play her song of delight through you . . . This is your moment . . . (extended pause) . . .

Now let your color, your friend, begin to leave you. It has done its work well. Let it pour out of your feet and wend its way toward an ocean of rainbow light . . . Gradually, slowly, at your own pace, let this color flow out of you, leaving you fresh and new. It has now completely left your head . . . now your shoulders and chest . . . and now it leaves your arms refreshed . . . It is gently leaving your stomach and back satisfied . . . departing from your abdomen and hips . . . going down through your legs, and finally completely out of the bottoms of your feet. Your color moves on to merge with the ocean, leaving you free to rest and breathe open, alive, and energetic.

*To discuss:*

What was your color? What healing effects did you experience from your color?

# IX. WHO AM I?

*For calm detachment and mental clarity*

*Speak slowly and allow participants time to contemplate these thoughts.*

Sitting with your spine erect and firm, yet comfortable, close your eyes and begin to observe your breath. Feel the rhythm of the breath as it flows in and out in an easy and natural way. Watch your breath entering and leaving your nose. Don't try to breathe in any particular way; let the breath flow at its own depth and pace. Just let the breath rise and fall as it wants to, and your only job is to observe it.

Notice how the breath forms and dissolves. See, too, if you can find the point at which the inbreath changes to become the outbreath . . . And then see if you can catch that subtle point where the breath stops going out and begins to return inward . . . For a little while, stay with your breath. See if you can keep your attention on its rhythm and on nothing else. As you stay with it, you will notice more and more subtle levels of the breath . . . You may find the breath becoming very quiet and almost still . . . Good.

Now ask yourself, "Who am *I?* . . . Who am *I?* . . . Who is it that says, 'I?' . . . Am I this body? Am I my arms or legs or heart? . . . No, not really . . . There is more to me than my body . . . I am told that there are no cells in my body more than a few years old . . . The cells are constantly dying and being replaced by new ones . . . If I am my body, then I was the cells that were in the body a few years ago . . . But they are not here, and *I* am still here . . . *I* must be more than just a body . . . But *who?* . . . *Who* am I?" . . .

Now observe your ears hearing, and notice it is the *ears* that hear, and then send *you* the information . . . For a few moments, don't identify with the ears. If you hear a sound, let it be the ears that hear, and *you* that observes what the ears hear . . . "So I am not my ears, and in the same way neither am I the rest of my body, but who am 'I'?"

"Perhaps I am my emotions . . . But that can't be, either, as my emotions change so much. They come and go, too. Happiness comes and goes. Sadness comes, and it goes. There is joy, and sorrow. Annoyance, and enthusiasm. Which of these emotions is real? All of them? . . . None of them? . . . And who is it that is feeling these emotions? We say, 'I feel happy' or 'I feel peaceful.' Who is the 'I' that is feeling happy or peaceful? Certainly there are times when I feel no emotion at all . . . and yet, at such times, I am . . . So I must not be my emotions, either. Who, then, am 'I'?"

"Perhaps I am my thoughts . . . But the thoughts come and go even more rapidly than the emotions! . . . There is a steady stream of thoughts that just keep changing . . . Certainly I can't be any one of these, for they seem to disappear in an instant! And then, too, sometimes I say 'I changed my mind.' . . . Then I certainly can't be my mind, if there is an *I* that changes the mind. *Who* is it that changed the mind? I don't say 'I changed myself'; *I* changed *my* mind. So the idea that 'I am my thoughts' must go, too."

Now come into a clear space, as if you are rising above your thoughts . . . As you rise, see the space between your thoughts increase, so you are observing your thoughts forming and dissolving, coming and going like fluffy clouds on a spring day . . .

Rest easily in this free and boundless space, not bound by any experience. You are free, now, above your body, your emotions, and your mind, above the coming and going of all forms. Just you. Just "I." Just being . . . Above all forms . . . Beyond all changes . . . Above even the thought of "I," for "I" is just a thought, too . . .

# X. GUIDING STAR
## *To nurture trust and self-esteem.*

See yourself lying on the side of a grassy hill on a warm summer's night. Your body is nestled so comfortably in the soft, plush grass, and you feel as if you could just lie here forever under the starlit sky.

As you gaze up at the millions of shining lights in the heavens, you notice that one star seems to be twinkling just a little brighter than the others; its light is just a little clearer, and its rays a little stronger. You are fascinated by this one special star, and after a few moments you begin to feel that it is twinkling right at you, as if it has a special message for you, as if it wants to shine right on you. The light from the star is becoming brighter and brighter now, and as you look at this star it seems to be coming closer to you.

To your happy surprise, you see the star actually *is* moving toward you, leaving its spot in the distant heavens and wending its way toward the earth. It is coming closer and closer, and you feel so happy to see it slowly, gently approaching your peaceful place. It is now floating very near, until it is just a few hundred feet from you. It is a pulsating blue and white light, and it seems to shine with a light that comes from a distant yet very familiar source. You realize now that the star is your friend, and that it has come for the very special purpose of being with you.

You welcome your star as it approaches, hovering just a few feet in front of you. Its light is soothing and soft, and it makes you happy just to be near it. Now, to your delight, the star comes right up to you . . . and it enters the center of your chest. As this twinkling light lovingly settles inside of you, you can feel waves and waves of peace emanating through your body, emotions, and mind. This is one of the most wonderful feelings you have ever experienced. You just want this starlight to stay with you forever. Now the star is expanding to fill your entire body, until every atom of you is vibrating in harmony with the blue and white waves.

Now feel a breeze of light beneath you . . . You are being lifted up by a cushion of soft light, rising off the ground . . . As you rise higher and higher, ascending into the heavens, look down upon the earth and see a tapestry of rich colors . . . Rise higher, now, and see the hills, the valleys, and the streams. It is a magnificent sight to behold. As you keep rising, the whole earth comes into perspective, and you are awed at the brilliance of the blues, the browns, and the whites. See how full and round is this majestic planet, one living organism . . .

Now go even higher, until you can see the whole solar system in its glorious precision . . . Go farther, and see the Milky Way, breathtaking beyond compare . . . Now keep going on your cushion of starry light, until you come to the center of the universe. It is as if all creation is breathing before you. From your still center, look at the perfection of the whole universe. See the stars, the planets, and all life, and feel your deep connection to everything that lives. Now you see that all of the universe is alive, and you are alive with it. You are in everything and everything is within you. The universe is a great living being, and you live at its center . . . (*extended pause*) . . .

Now with this perfect awareness begin to once again take form as a star and travel back through the heavens . . . See the Milky Way, the solar system, and the earth. You know these scenes; they are a part of you.

Now approach the earth, with its rich mountains and lush valleys. Your cushion of light is bringing you back to that grassy hill where your journey began. Enjoy yourself as you slowly descend toward the plush green grass. As you touch down and feel the firmness of the earth beneath you, feel a twinkling energy all through your system. Now feel a burst of light in your chest, and see a blue and white star, twinkling ever-so-gently, emerge from your center. See the star float to a point a few feet from you, and watch it begin to ascend into the heavens. As it rises, see it stop for a moment, shine on you, and wink . . . You smile as you receive its message of loving guidance. Watch it rise slowly and steadily back to its place in the starry sky. Look again and see all the stars shining in the heavens, with one star twinkling just a bit brighter than the others, on this warm and pleasant summer starlit night.

# XI. HELPING HANDS

*To enhance the quality and success of human services.*

This image is a powerful one, especially valuable for teachers, doctors and nurses, counselors, therapists, and all whose work includes a sincere desire to help other people.

For this visualization, sit up with your back straight and your feet flat on the floor. Place your hands on your thighs with the palms facing upward and fingers spread slightly apart.

Visualize above your head a great funnel, or vortex of golden light. It is like the upper half of an hourglass. The top of it extends far above you, and it seems to be reaching down from an infinite ocean of bright energy. This energy pours directly into the top of your head, and your body is like the bottom of the hourglass.

See and feel this golden energy flowing slowly and steadily into and through your body. First it illuminates your head, softening your thoughts and balancing the energies in both sides of your brain and nervous system. It is a soothing, peaceful energy. You welcome it, for you know that it is helping you.

Let the light, like a substance, flow down through your shoulders and arms, as if this intelligent energy knows exactly where to go. Feel that this energy wants to be put to good use. Let it pour into your hands and fingers, making them bright and radiant.

Let yourself be open to receive the brightness of this power, and let it flow down through your chest and your torso. Feel how every organ wants to receive this positive energy, and to absorb it. Visualize how your nervous system is being energized in a positive and useful way, and balance is coming about in your whole self.

This pleasant light continues, now, through your abdomen and flows easily and naturally down through your hips and legs. This life force completely restores aliveness and alertness to all parts of your body. It is very good. Let it flow into your feet and toes, going completely to the tips of your toes. Feel the grounding effect of the energy. With your feet flat on the floor, feel connected to the earth, solid and firm. In this energy your actions are sure and steady.

Now return your awareness to the upper parts of your body, especially your arms and your hands. Feel that you are a vessel, a channel for this life force to flow through you. See that there is an infinite resource of energy above your head, and it is willing to let you use as much of it as you like, in whatever way you wish.

Pay special attention to how that energy flows from above your head, down through your arms, and out your hands. Your hands are taking on a special glow, a power to give this energy out. Keep thinking of your hands and see that with each breath they become brighter and brighter. Now watch this light begin to ray out from your fingertips. See your fingers and palms emanating a strong power, one which is good and positive. Let that light become more and more brilliant, until you feel that whatever or whoever your hands touch would receive this energy and feel better because of it . . .

Visualize placing your hands on different objects in your life. Start with some living plants or flowers . . . See how they respond to this energy . . . (extended pause) . . . Next, mentally place them on your car and your home . . . If you work with your hands in a craft or art, visualize waves of creative energy being poured into your work. Watch a mental movie of yourself at work and see your hands being guided to perform just the right movements at just the right time. Feel as if you could breathe life into your work, and see the most wonderful results of the work of your hands. Begin to see pictures and images of talented and unique craftsmanship. See how successful your work is, and feel grateful for these excellent results. . .

If you work with people, visualize yourself standing in your office or classroom or wherever your service is done. Now mentally lift up your hands and see the entire room becoming filled with golden light. It is becoming more and more powerful, until the room is completely filled with a healing light. Feel that whoever walks into this room will immediately be filled with a deep sense of peace and well-being. Feel that you have created an atmosphere that will help every person you serve . . .

Now think of one of your students, clients, or patients, whoever comes into your mind first. See this person with a bright, shining face, without problems . . . See them happy, whole and satisfied with themselves. See the best of their qualities and magnify these qualities in your mind until all you see in them is their positive, good, successful self. Imagine what it would be like if your work with them were a complete success . . . Imagine that all you want for them has come to pass, even beyond your expectations. Fantasize and exaggerate in your mind all the good things that you would like to see come about as a result of your work with them . . . (extended pause) . . .

Now feel satisfied about yourself in the same way. Visualize all the success that you would like to see come to pass in your personal work. See all the best things that could happen to you. See all of the strong qualities in yourself. Exaggerate and expand all of your special abilities, and know that they are real. Know, too, that you have an important contribution to make in your work, and that you are here for a good purpose. Many people are being helped by your work, and your projects are gifts you are giving to the world . . .

Now visualize yourself lying in bed before going to sleep. As you mentally review your day, let a feeling of deep satisfaction well up within you. See that all you have done is good and that other people's lives are better because you affected them in a positive way. You can be well satisfied with yourself . . .

*Sufficient pause . . . then return awareness to room.*

25

# XII. CIRCLE OF LOVE
## *For healing relationships.*

Take this lovely scene in mind: Imagine yourself standing on a plateau, a magnificent site overlooking an ocean . . . It's just before sunset on a pleasantly warm summer's day. The pastel tones on the horizon are pink and amber and tangerine, and deep within you there is a sense of coming home.

Think now of someone, a friend, a companion, a teacher, from whom you have felt the most love in your life. Perhaps it is someone dear to you now; or it might be a friend who has passed on; or perhaps it is a spiritual guide who loves you without condition or expectation . . . Let it be someone who gives you all of their love in a way that you know is real. Imagine that he or she is standing before you, as both of you overlook this great panorama of tranquility . . .

Face this special person now and take their hands. Look into his or her eyes and begin to feel waves of complete acceptance, as if that person is saying, "You're beautiful just as you are . . . You're *you* and I love you" . . . In this moment — this very special moment — you are as fulfilled as you could possibly be . . . (*extended pause*) . . .

Now imagine standing all around you, in a great circle of love, all those who have ever loved you, who have shared their heart with you in some way, those who have made your journey through life worthwhile. As you look at their smiling, shining faces, go back in memory and remember what a help their caring and kindness has been for you. Recall their sensitivity and their warmth, their help and their understanding. See all of them standing around you now, peaceful and loving, with their arms open toward you in total acceptance, for they love you still . . . (*extended pause*) . . .

Go to them now, go to each one and embrace them . . . Look into their eyes and without a word say, "Thank you . . . Your love has meant so much to me." . . . As you go around the circle, realize that no matter what has happened in your life, no matter what you have done, you could never lose their love, nor could you ever be unloved. And feel how glad they are that you have accepted their love for, in truth, all they want for you is your own happiness . . . As you go to each one, a feeling of deep happiness wells up within you, and the light within the circle is even more beautiful and healing than the light from the setting sun itself . . . This is a magical moment for you . . .

Now see more people joining the ranks of this circle of love, perhaps some people who you did not expect to be here, but who you now realize love you. You see some people whom you feel you may have hurt in some way along the path of your life . . . Yet they stand, too, with their arms open and their hearts aglow in forgiveness . . . See who they are and awaken to their love for you . . . (*extended pause*) . . .

Now see even more people coming into the circle: those who you feel have hurt you or been unkind to you . . . See who they are . . . They have come to the circle to ask for your forgiveness . . . It is so easy to forgive in this circle, so easy to let go in this atmosphere of warm understanding . . . Yes, of course you can forgive . . . What could offer you more peace than the shining love that you feel

26

now? . . . Release any hurts or bitterness, and replace it with the pastel light of the setting sun . . . *(extended pause)* . . .

Now with your love complete and your feelings resolved, visualize this entire scene as if you are looking down upon it from the sky . . . See the circle of love on this picturesque plateau overlooking the ocean . . . Now you are as great as the sky itself, and you are as whole as all that is good. Take the entire scene into your heart. Every person you see, every feeling that is flowing through you . . . every ray of light . . . and every fulfilled dream is now within you, for in truth you know that love *is* the greatest of all . . .

*Allow time for transition.*

# NOTES

## PLEASE SEND ME THE FOLLOWING:

| Title | Price | Qty. | Total |
|---|---|---|---|
| **BOOKS** | | | |
| Companions of the Heart | $19.95 | | |
| Dare To Be Yourself | 11.95 | | |
| The Dragon Doesn't Live Here Anymore | 9.95 | | |
| Have You Hugged a Monster Today? | 3.95 | | |
| The Healing of the Planet Earth | 9.95 | | |
| Joy Is My Compass | 9.95 | | |
| The Peace That You Seek | 13.95 | | |
| Rising in Love | 8.95 | | |
| Setting the Seen | 2.95 | | |
| **CASSETTES** | | | |
| Deep Relaxation | 9.95 | | |
| Eden Morning | 9.95 | | |
| I Believe in You | 9.95 | | |
| Miracle Mountain (4-cassette album) | 29.95 | | |
| Peace | 9.95 | | |
| **VIDEO** | | | |
| Dare To Be Yourself | 39.95 | | |

Subtotal ___

WA Residents Add 8.2% sales tax ___

Shipping: Add 10% of subtotal ($2 minimum) ___

**SHIP TO:**          TOTAL ___

Name (please print): _____

Street Address: _____

City:_____ State:_____ Zip:_____

Phone (day): (_____) _____ (evening): (_____) _____

***ORDER TOLL-FREE*** 1(800)462-3013 (Mon-Fri 9AM-5PM Pacific Time)
Visa, MasterCard, American Express. *Toll-free number for orders only.*

**PAYMENT:**
☐ Check or Money Order
☐ Visa  ☐ MasterCard  ☐ American Express

Card #: _____ Exp. Date: _____

Print Cardholder's Name:_____

Cardholder's Signature:_____

Mail check or money order payable in U.S. funds to:
ALAN COHEN PUBLICATIONS • P.O. Box 98509 • Des Moines, WA 98198